Robin McKie

Nuclear Energy

Macdonald

A MACDONALD BOOK

First published in 1984 by
Macdonald & Co. (Publishers) Ltd
London & Sydney

Reprinted 1985, 1987

© Robin McKie 1984

Macdonald & Co. (Publishers) Ltd
Greater London House
Hampstead Road
London NW1 7QX
A BPCC plc company

Printed and bound in Great Britain by
Blantyre Printing Ltd, London and Glasgow

BRITISH LIBRARY
CATALOGUING IN PUBLICATION DATA

McKie, Robin
    Nuclear energy. – (Debates series)
    1. Atomic power – Juvenile literature
    I. Title II. Series
    621.48   TK9148
ISBN 0-356-10138-X

7.99

Contents

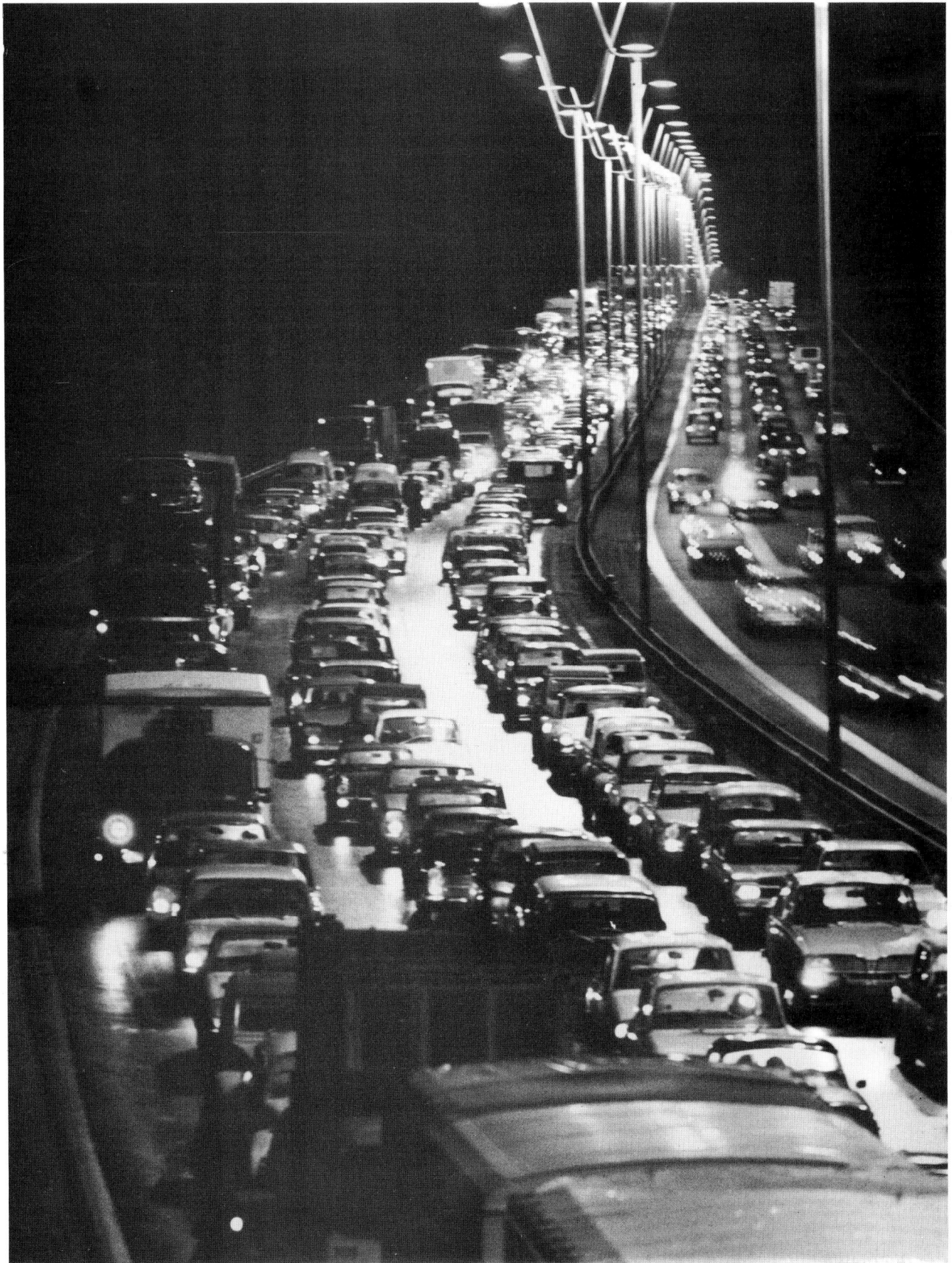

A world without energy?

Modern civilization depends on energy. Without it our lives would be reduced to the level of a caveman's. We would have no way of running cars, trains, or planes. We would have nothing to power the tractors, drills and cranes we need to make buildings. We would have no electricity for televisions, radios or telephones, for cooking or for lighting. Without wood, we would not even be able to light fires for warmth. Our days would be spent huddled in caves with only raw meat and vegetables for food. This is a stark picture, but it shows just how vital energy is to our lives.

Historical perspective Human progress has been closely linked to discovering new ways to make power. At first we could only burn wood for heat. Later we learned to use coal. Then we made steam and began an industrial revolution that launched us towards our modern technological society. Since then we have developed many other sources of energy – including oil, gas, and nuclear and solar power.

But the world's appetite for power is also increasing – possibly too rapidly for us to manage. Since 1900 energy consumption has increased tenfold – and that rise is bound to continue, scientists and politicians warn us. By the year 2000, there will be 6.5 billion people on Earth – many of them living in slums or other impoverished areas.

The need for energy We need plentiful energy to combat that poverty. It will help people keep warm, keep clean, cook food, run industries and make things. 'Power consumption and standard of living go hand in

> *'There is no substitute for energy; the whole edifice of modern life is built upon it.'*
> E. F. Schumacher, author and economist

hand,' the eminent American scientist, Professor Gerard O'Neill believes. 'Whether the turn of the century finds our civilization in a downward slide towards poverty, accompanied by warfare over the remaining energy sources, or at the dawn of a better age will depend on our developing sources of energy for Earth.'

Scientists disagree about exactly how much energy we will need in the future, while others question whether we can continue to use traditional power sources for much longer. But no-one doubts that our energy needs will continue to grow, while present available resources decline. And this is at the heart of the debate about nuclear energy.

> *'Energy is more important than money.'*
> Sir Fred Hoyle, physicist

> *'Back to the Ice Age – no thanks! We need nuclear power.'*
> Pro-nuclear car sticker

Opposite The fabric of life as we know it depends on energy. Without ways of controlling energy, we would have neither cars nor electricity, for example.

Oil wells are the world's energy lifeline. This lake in Venezuela has been exploited for half a century, but the oil is now running out.

Running out of fuel?

Every day, the world uses up more than 10,000 million litres of oil – as well as large amounts of natural gas and coal. Inevitably, reserves of these fuels must run out, and many scientists fear we are fast approaching that day. We must act now, they say, or face a return to the Stone Age.

How real is the threat? In the confusing welter of claims and counterclaims, it is difficult to be certain just how close we are to disaster. Geologists, for example, still do not know, and have no means of calculating, exactly how much coal, gas and oil is left on Earth. At the moment, they are still finding new oil wells and coal reserves, although the rate of discoveries has slowed down in recent years. Nevertheless, there are still large areas of the world not yet prospected.

Similarly, economists are unsure how much energy we will need in future. If countries do well, they will need more power for new industries. If they do badly, they will need less.

However, all are agreed that if demand rises, oil – the most versatile and useful of fuels – will run out very quickly. Some predictions suggest this could happen within 20 years. At best reserves can only last another 80 years. Similarly our stocks of coal are not limitless and will run out, some say in 50 years, others in 1,000. Gas, too, will only last another 25 to 150 years.

'The prospects for oil, natural gas and coal afford little optimism about our energy future,' warned one group of American economists recently.

It is a bleak picture, especially for oil. A relatively light liquid, oil can be easily moved from wells to refineries and this makes it an ideal fuel for cars and planes. Running aircraft on uranium or pumping coal through pipelines would not be very easy!

Living without oil We clearly need other energy sources to free our last precious drops of oil for the tasks to which it alone is suited. As researchers Daniel Deudney and Christopher Flavin said about oil in a recent report for the Worldwatch Institute: 'Reliance on such an extremely concentrated resource is an invitation to crisis'.

Many different and extreme courses of action have been proposed. We could build several thousand nuclear power stations to generate electricity, and use liquefied coal and our last oil for transport fuel. Or we could drastically reduce our use of energy, develop reusable power sources such as solar, wind and wave technology, and recycle all industrial products as far as possible.

The trouble is, as the magazine *Newsweek* warned, 'most debt-strapped developing nations can no longer afford the huge start-up costs of importing or developing nuclear energy' even if they wanted to.

Using alternative sources of energy is equally unlikely to meet their growing needs, however. Balancing these two courses of action is going to be tricky, and future generations will have to be the judges of how well we managed to respond to the problem.

> **'The world has an abundance of energy.'**
> *Centre for Energy Studies*

'Contrary to an influential belief – we do not have time. There is no practical alternative to nuclear energy.' *Sir Alan Cottrell, scientist*

How much energy do we need?

Across America, a new type of wilderness park has taken shape. Filled with abandoned steel and concrete structures, they are the remnants of nuclear power stations recently scrapped in the wake of a widespread slump in US reactor building.

In the early 1970s American generating companies were ordering 30 to 40 new reactors a year. Then decline set in and, by 1978, orders had dropped to zero. None have been placed since then – while 37 old reactors have been abandoned and construction of a further 15 new ones has been suspended.

Learning to live with less energy This decline has occurred for several reasons – including growing public concern about reactor safety. Another major cause has been a world economic slump that has forced companies out of business, cutting demand for electricity.

For instance, in the United States – the world's greatest user of energy – demand for electricity rose dramatically in the 1950s and '60s. By 1980 it was only increasing by 1.7 per cent a year, and by 0.3 per cent in 1981. Then, in 1982, it actually shrank by 2.3 per cent – the first decline in the use of power since the end of the Second World War.

But there has been a further, more interesting cause. Suddenly the western world seems to have learned how to manage with less energy. Rising oil prices forced many companies and governments to realize they had been wasting power, and many began ambitious conservation programmes.

One of the most radical of these was implemented in the United States by its President, Jimmy Carter. His measures included: speed restrictions on US highways (cars use less fuel per mile at lower speeds); the creation of energy 'security' corporations to develop oil substitutes such as liquefied coal; and increased support for public transport systems, which use less energy per passenger than private cars. Other industrialized countries adopted similar policies.

By 1981, the West had become a fifth more energy efficient than it had been in 1973. Airlines used planes that needed less fuel, car manufacturers built more efficient vehicle engines, hotels cut air conditioning and heating bills, and house builders improved insulation in homes.

Rich and poor All this is very good news, but most scientists and economists agree that these improvements will not turn the tide. We will still be using up unrenewable resources at a very fast rate. And the West – Britain, the United States, Canada, Australia, much of Europe and a few other countries – will still be soaking up far more than their fair share of the world's energy.

This disparity is clearly illustrated when comparing different countries' energy use per head of population. A citizen of the United States consumes the equivalent of about 11.6 tonnes of coal a year; a Canadian, about 10.7; a Briton, 5.4; a Mexican, 1.3; an Indian 0.18; and an Ethopian, 0.035.

> 'We have time. We can at present make more electricity than we need.' The Sunday Times, 12 December 1976

The poor, developing nations of Africa, Asia and South America – which use only a fraction of the energy that the West consumes at present – are beginning to demand more energy, to enable them to industrialize and struggle out of poverty.

'Improvements in fuel efficiency can only slightly reduce increases in fuel and energy demands,' warned Fritz Schumacher, the energy expert who predicted many of the world's present energy problems. The energy crisis will not be shrugged aside very easily.

Opposite Nuclear energy – the end of the golden years. An abandoned reactor in Buffalo, New York.

9

Power from

Our bodies, and the world about us, are made of atoms – tiny particles that are invisible to the naked eye. The existence of atoms was first suggested by the ancient Greeks but was not proved until the last century. Then it was found that atoms of the same element

> 'The energy produced by the breaking down of the atom is a very poor kind of thing. Anyone who expects a source of power from the transformation of these atoms is talking moonshine.' Lord Ernest Rutherford

(such as hydrogen, oxygen, iron and others) are identical, and that chemical compounds are made of combinations of these atoms.

The birth of nuclear physics At first scientists thought atoms were indivisible. Then, in 1917, the renowned New Zealand physicist, Ernest Rutherford, showed that the atom itself is made up of even smaller particles. An atom consists of tiny electrons which surround a larger central nucleus (later proved to be made up of protons and neutrons).

This discovery was made by a scientist generally regarded as one of the greatest experimenters of all time. Yet even Rutherford failed to see the practical significance of his work. He rejected any suggestion that the

> 'Atomic energy will prove to be the most important scientific development since the discovery of fire.' Government report, 1953

energies of the atom could ever be released and put to use. Nuclear physics remained a theoretical science only.

Splitting the atom In the 1930s, scientists realized that the atoms of very heavy elements – particularly uranium – were unstable, and that under certain conditions could disintegrate to produce energy.

It was found that uranium atoms all have 92 protons in their nucleii, but that they do not all have the same number of neutrons. Some uranium atoms have 146, others only 143. The difference turned out to be crucial.

Uranium with 146 neutrons is called uranium 238 (92 protons plus 146 neutrons equals 238, its atomic weight). This type of uranium is quite stable and common. But the other form – uranium 235 – has a very special property: it breaks down when hit by another neutron in way that supports a self-sustaining reaction called 'fission'.

During fission a lot of atomic debris flies out. Energy is also produced and so are extra neutrons. These neutrons then hit other uranium atoms which in turn break down to produce more energy and more neutrons. These then hit further uranium atoms – and so a chain reaction is set off.

This chain reaction produces a great deal of energy. Nuclear bombs – like the one which destroyed the city of Hiroshima in 1945 with an explosive force of 60,000 tonnes of TNT – are produced in this way.

But the reaction can also be controlled – by placing the uranium inside other materials, such as graphite, which absorb some of the neutrons. Energy and heat are then released in a manageable way – which is what happens in a nuclear reactor.

an atom

Right The nuclear chain reaction – a neutron splits a uranium atom (top left), breaking it apart, and releasing other neutrons. These neutrons break open other uranium atoms which in turn release more neutrons – and so the reaction rapidly multiplies.

Below A nuclear bomb blast – a dramatic demonstration of the mighty powers locked inside an atom.

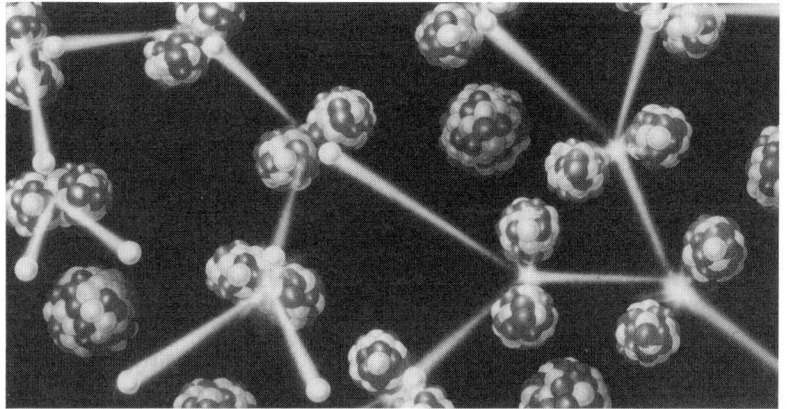

Nuclear reactors

Nuclear reactors are extremely sophisticated devices and cost a great deal of money to build. In particular, much effort is spent on designing and installing systems which will prevent harmful radiation from leaking from uranium fuel and its fission by-products – for in sufficiently high doses, radiation can kill or can cause serious illnesses such as cancer.

How a nuclear reactor works Inside the reactor, uranium is first placed inside long canisters, and these rods are then slotted into a large lump of graphite, called the core – along with an extra control rod. This control rod is usually made of a substance such as boron which absorbs neutrons like a sponge. As the control rod is slowly removed from the core, a nuclear chain reaction starts up and heat is produced. If too much heat is generated, then the control rod is simply returned, more neutrons are absorbed and the reaction slows down.

To take away the heat, a gas or liquid – known as a coolant – is pumped through the core. The coolant gets heated – to between 250 and 600 deg C – and is then used to turn water into very hot steam. The steam drives a turbine which produces electricity.

Radiation The entire nuclear reactor apart from the turbines is usually covered by a giant protective shield or dome. This is to hold in any radiation which has not been contained by the core. Most radiation is absorbed in the core, but some, known as gamma rays, can travel through several metres of concrete. As a result the reactor is surrounded by a giant protective layer of material – usually concrete or heavy-welded steel.

Design variations This basic design applies to all nuclear reactors, but there are minor variations. Some reactors, particularly British ones, use carbon dioxide under heavy pressure as a coolant; others – particularly American and French ones – use water; some even use liquid sodium. Similarly there are different fuels – uranium metal, uranium oxide, or even mixtures of uranium and plutonium, which is itself a by-product of uranium-burning reactors. Each variation has advantages and disadvantages.

A PWR (pressurized water reactor) – one of the commonest types of nuclear reactor worldwide. It is operated by removing control rods from the fuel elements, so starting up a chain reaction. Water is pumped in (from the left) and comes out hot. Inside the steam generator, the very hot pressurized water (at around 300 deg C) is used to make steam that drives turbines.

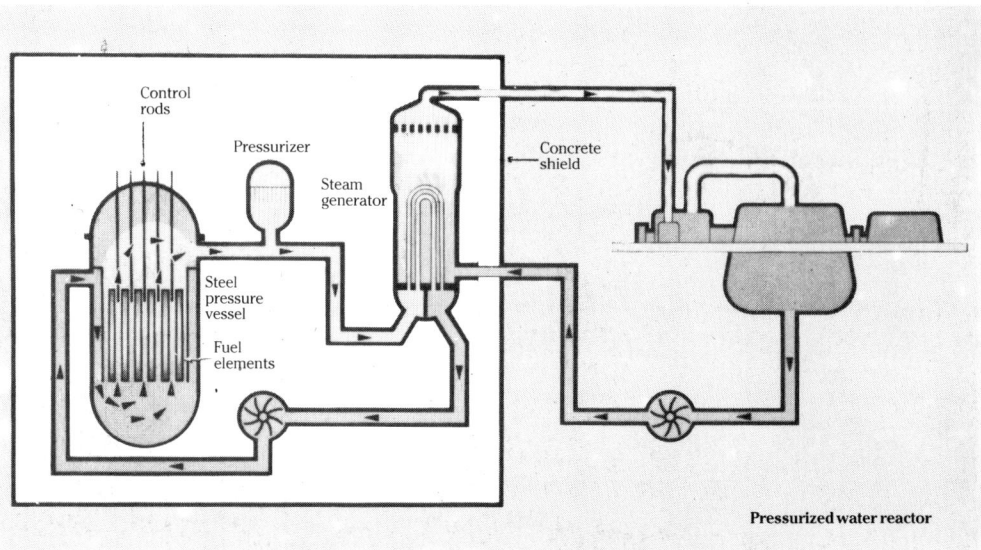

Control rods

Pressurizer

Steam generator

Concrete shield

Steel pressure vessel

Fuel elements

Pressurized water reactor

Uranium

Uranium is a hard, metallic element found in minerals such as pitchblende – which occurs in the United States, Canada, Australia and Africa. However, this ore is mostly made up of the slightly heavier type – or isotope – uranium 238. Less than one per cent is uranium 235, the only isotope that will support a chain reaction.

Enriching uranium Increasing levels of uranium 235 is known as 'enrichment' – a tricky and expensive business. The most common method is to force the uranium through very thin, porous membranes. The lighter uranium 235 passes through slightly faster than the uranium 238. There are only very slight differences in the speed, however, and in order to produce fuel that is more than 95 per cent uranium 235, this operation must be repeated several thousand times. Fortunately most reactors use fuel that is only three or four per cent uranium 235 – which requires less preparation.

Other enrichment techniques involve using spinning centrifuges which force the heavier uranium 238 further to the edges of circular chambers. Scientists are also working on ways to enrich uranium with lasers – although this research is surrounded by a great deal of secrecy because of its military implications.

The turbine hall of a nuclear plant – where steam is used to generate electricity.

'A nuclear reactor is an incredibly complex machine. It is like building a giant Swiss watch.' US nuclear engineer

At 5.40 a.m. on 10 October 1957, fire was discovered inside a reactor at the Windscale nuclear centre in Cumbria, recently renamed Sellafield. Uranium fuel and cladding was ablaze and was melting, causing temperatures to soar dangerously inside the core.

For more than a day, engineers and scientists battled to control the inferno and did not succeed until they managed to pump water into the reactor. Unfortunately they could not stop the release of a cloud of highly radioactive dust, and although much was trapped by the reactor's air filters, some did escape.

> 'A nuclear explosion is no more feasible in a nuclear reactor than it is from chewing pickled cucumber or gum.' Lord Rothschild

The consequences were deadly – for an estimated 33 people in the surrounding countryside were killed by escaping radioactivity. This is a statistical estimate, however. No one died instantly, nor do we know who they might be. Indeed, most will have taken years to contract cancers or other radiation-caused diseases.

An isolated incident? The Windscale fire remains the world's worst recorded nuclear accident and to nuclear opponents it was a warning that other reactors may one day cause far greater devastation.

'Nuclear power threatens the health, freedom and safety of everyone ... and the lives of generations to come,' states the environ-

> 'Nuclear power is in many ways a technological Vietnam.' John Abotts and Ralph Nader in The Menace of Atomic Energy

mental group Friends of the Earth. 'It is unique in the hazards it poses.'

This claim is rejected by nuclear power supporters who see the Windscale fire as an isolated, rare event. Nuclear plants have excellent safety records, they say, and have been responsible for few deaths – certainly far, far fewer than car or air crash fatalities which now get relatively little public attention.

'The hard facts are that nuclear energy up till now has been extremely safe,' says Sir Alan Cottrell, scientific adviser. 'The safety record of the nuclear industry has been almost immaculate.'

Covering up? Nevertheless, there have been some very close calls. For instance, in 1961, a small US Army reactor in Idaho exploded killing three technicians; in 1966, a larger reactor in Detroit almost blew up, which would have caused wide devastation; and in 1979, a near-disaster at the Three Mile Island reactor in Pennsylvania led to widespread local evacuations.

These examples only fuel general public fears about possible catastrophes at nuclear plants – and lead to allegations that the authorities are trying to cover up even greater risks.

Oddly, nuclear supporters also condemn the industry's secretiveness. 'Nuclear authorities have alienated many people by their secretiveness, bland pronouncements and superior "Daddy knows best" attitudes,' said Sir Alan Cottrell. But then he and his associates believe more openness would only confirm that nuclear power is safe.

Others believe that one of the greatest problems with nuclear power is the impossibility of accurately assessing the potential dangers when they can take so long to manifest themselves. We simply have not had nuclear energy for long enough, they say.

The safe atom?

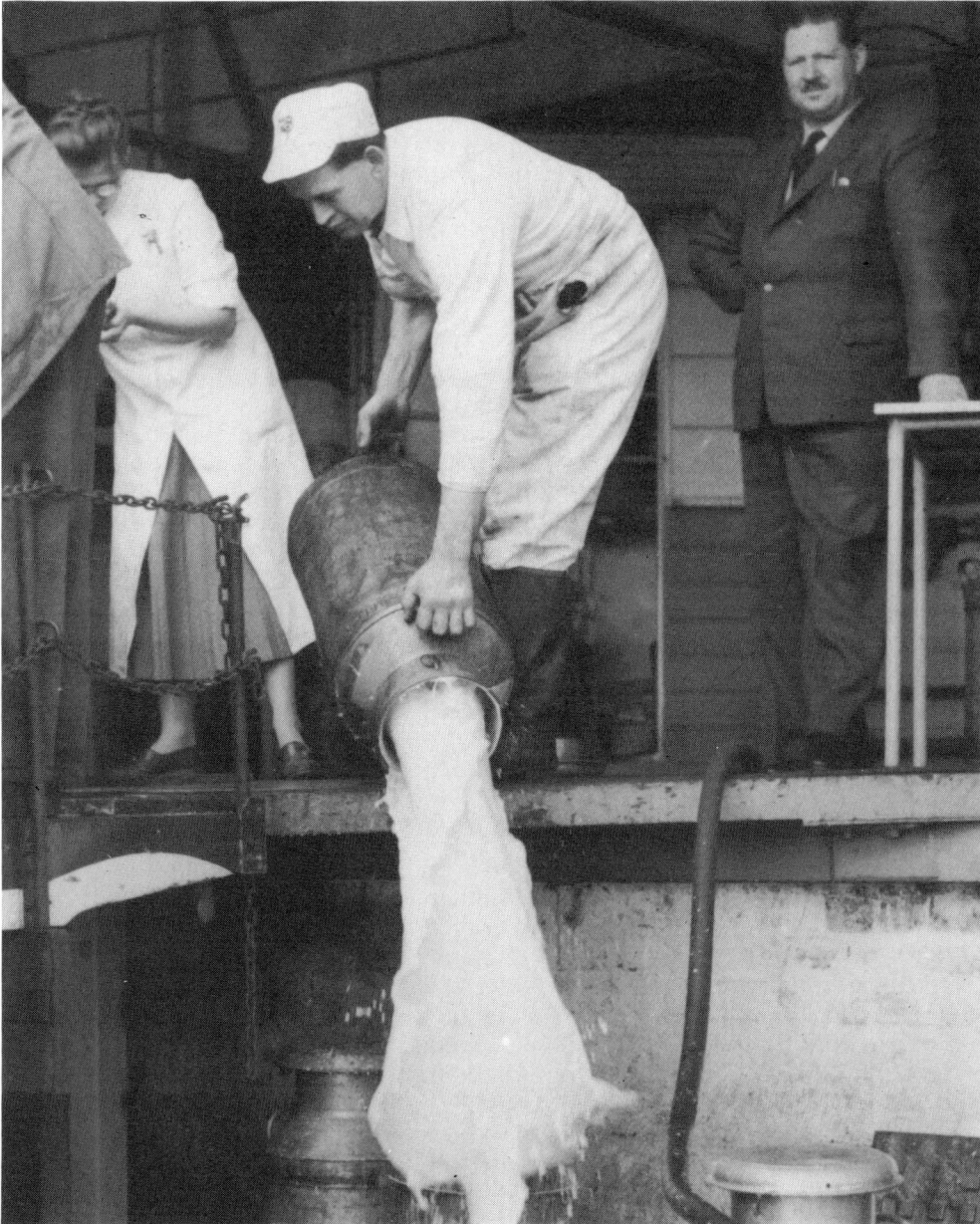

The aftermath of the Windscale fire – all milk from cows grazing within 200 miles of the plant had to be poured away.

How dangerous is radiation?

Very heavy elements, like uranium, are unstable and can break apart. When this happens they emit radiation. Many natural substances are weakly radioactive, but some nuclear reactor by-products give off intense radiation.

Just how this might affect a human is still a highly controversial issue – despite considerable research in recent years. However, it is not disputed that too much radiation will ultimately kill a person.

A question of degree? In a bid to quantify the problem, radiologists have developed a measure of radiation called a 'rem'. They reckon a single dose of 600 rems is fatal, that 100 will cause radiation sickness and that 0.5 is the maximum annual dose to which people should be exposed. Above these levels, the body's complex molecules can be disrupted. Tumours can be caused, blood diseases like leukaemia can be produced, and even reproductive organs can be affected.

However scientists still disagree about the exact doses which might produce such carried across the country or is dumped at sea or below ground.

Indeed, because radiation is invisible and undetectable, it can arouse particularly vivid fears. As one expert said: 'In insidious silence, radiation can produce medical effects of the kind most dreaded by people – cancer in the living body and genetic mutilations in future generations.'

It sounds alarming, but let us also remember that we are always exposed to radiation – from cosmic rays, from rocks such as granite, and from X-rays used by dentists and doctors. Each year, it is estimated we receive an annual dose of 0.12 rems of radiation – and only 0.1 per cent of that is thought to come from nuclear discharges.

If true, this makes smoking or car driving infinitely more dangerous than living near a nuclear reactor. However, there are scientists who believe this is a complacent view. They argue that the body's reaction to radiation is so delicate that any increase in levels, no matter how small, could seriously and even fatally affect our health.

> 'It is possible that the degree of radiological safety we demand is incompatible with the existence of a viable nuclear industry.'
>
> Dr Irving Leach, New York Medical Centre

effects. In fact, some question if there can ever be a safe dose of radiation at all. 'Any dose of radiation is an overdose,' the Nobel-prize-winning biologist, Dr George Wald, once stated.

These arguments are important when discussing nuclear power, for its fuel cycle can lead to many dangers of exposure – no matter how small. Workers who mine uranium or reprocess spent fuel are affected – and so might be the public when that spent fuel is

Opposite Keeping out radiation – nuclear workers have to wear complex, sealed suits to prevent contamination.

Right The Windscale reprocessing plant – situated in the tranquil Cumbrian countryside – is the resting place for nearly all the radioactive waste generated by British reactors.

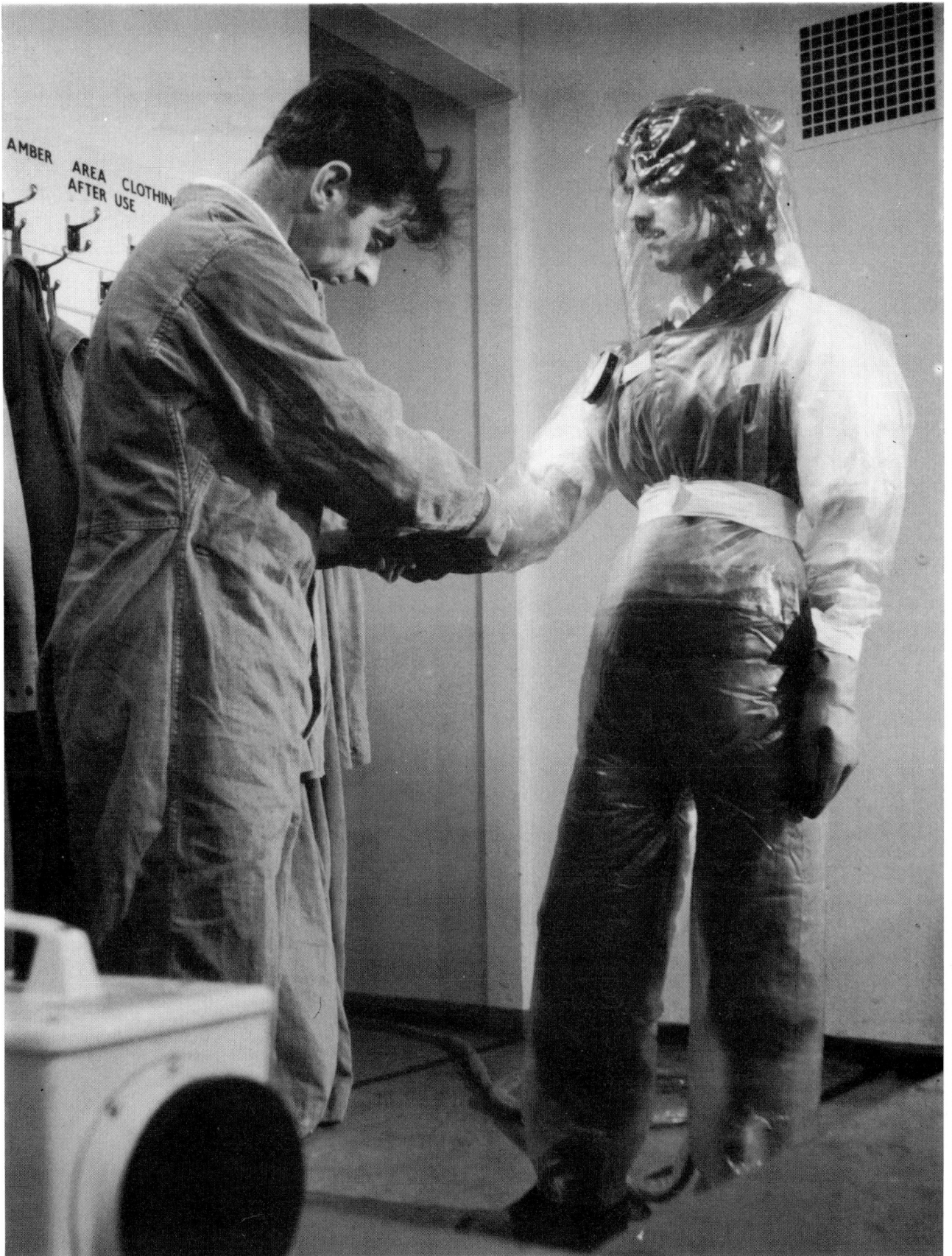

AMBER AREA CLOTHING AFTER USE

17

The human factor?

An accident at a nuclear plant – like any other mishap – can usually be squarely blamed on human error. But mistakes with reactors can have particularly destructive consequences, so great effort has to be made to reduce such risks as much as possible.

As a result, nuclear engineers have designed plants with hundreds of different safety systems, many of which duplicate each other.

inspection – using a candle for light! In the process he set off a blaze that spread round the plant, lasted seven hours, knocked out five emergency core-cooling systems, and put the station out of action for 18 months, at a final cost of 40 million dollars.

Design faults But operators and workmen are not necessarily the only culprits. Sometimes over-elaborate safety designs or bad

'If anything can go wrong, it will go wrong.' Murphy's Law

To err is human? 'Between paper and practice stand people,' says Sir Alan Cottrell. 'People who – in the nuclear industry – weld up steel structures, fit and test valves and pumps, load and unload fuel rods, check the quality of materials, and components, read instruments and press buttons in control rooms.'

And like other people, these technicians and workers sometimes cut corners, and make judgments about vague instructions in either a satisfactory or an unsatisfactory way. The results can be alarming.

For instance, the Windscale fire was actually caused by a scientist raising power levels too quickly because he thought – in part as a result of poor reactor instrumentation – that the core temperature was too low.

More bizarre was an incident at the Brown's Ferry nuclear reactor in Alabama in 1975. There an electrician carried out a cable

construction can lead to accidents – such as the one at the Enrico Fermi reactor near Detroit. There part of a safety system – added at the last minute at the insistence of the atomic safety authorities – broke apart, and several pieces blocked the reactor's cooling system. The result was a near devastating meltdown of the plant.

And although the Three Mile Island accident (see overleaf) was largely blamed on human error, there was evidence that operators had been badly confused by over 100 alarm bells ringing simultaneously, and the multitude of dials and controls giving madly fluctuating readings.

Trying to design safe plants which at the same time can be easily operated, while causing only remote risks of accidents, is a difficult task. The nuclear industry believes it has overcome this problem. Opponents doubt if they ever can.

The control centre of a nuclear plant in Bulgaria. Amid such complexity, every instrument and connection must be carefully checked for errors that could lead to devastating accidents.

Three Mile Island –

'Wherever we looked, we found problems with the human beings who operate the plant, with the management that runs the key organization, and with the agency charged with assuring the plant's safety.' Report by the Kemeny committee

More than a year after the near calamitous meltdown of the Three Mile Island reactor, technicians still had to wear heavy protective clothing in order to check damage at the crippled plant.

an isolated incident?

At 4 a.m. on 28 March 1979, several pumps – which supplied water coolant to the nuclear reactor at Three Mile Island near Harrisburg in the United States – failed. On its own, this was not a serious problem, but combined with other reactor breakdowns, it led to an incident that would give the name of Three Mile Island worldwide notoriety.

What happened? Without a proper supply of coolant, the temperature of the water round the reactor began to rise – so an emergency valve automatically opened to release the pressure of steam. When it dropped, the valve should have shut again. Instead it jammed open, allowing precious coolant to evaporate from the reactor while there was no more to replace it. Mysteriously a panel light in the reactor control room indicated that the valve had shut – causing near-fatal confusion among operators.

As the coolant continued to boil off through the valve, water levels inside the reactor dropped. Within hours, the uranium fuel rods were exposed and temperatures rocketed. The fuel's alloy cladding began to melt and react with the steam, while the uranium inside began to buckle and melt. Puzzled operators were still unaware that coolant was boiling off and so kept turning off automatic emergency cooling systems which could have pumped in extra water.

'Had the valve closed as it was designed to do or if the control room operators had realized that a valve was stuck open and closed the back-up valve… the accident at Three Mile Island would have remained little more than a minor inconvenience,' the official accident report later concluded.

The damage, and the fears By the time nuclear experts had realized what the problem was and had rectified it, incalculable damage had been done – not just to the reactor, but to the nuclear industry itself.

Fears of a dangerous release of radioactivity led to panic among local citizens; US President Jimmy Carter launched a special investigation; and when a remote television survey of the core was later carried out, engineers found that it had been reduced to a pile of highly radioactive rubble. The whole area was unapproachable, and it will be years before anyone can even get near the reactor to dismantle it.

Some parts of the nuclear industry – such as the Atomic Industry Forum – argued that the incident still showed that reactors were basically safe. A serious accident had occurred, but it had been contained and no one had been hurt, after all.

However, a report – prepared for America's Nuclear Regulatory Commission – did not support this. It claimed that, on 28 March 1979, the Three Mile Island reactor had only been one hour away from the worst possible nuclear plant accident – a complete core meltdown.

Police block roads after radioactive material escapes from another US nuclear plant the Ginna reactor, in New York state.

Chernobyl – end of a dream?

The small town of Chernobyl stands 370 miles south of Moscow. Set in the heart of the Ukraine, Chernobyl was once an undistinguished Soviet provincial township. Today, it is synonymous with catastrophe – the result of an explosion. The blast, on 26 April 1986, was the world's worst nuclear disaster.

A radioactive cloud Most of the plant's stock of highly radioactive material was hurled into the atmosphere by the explosion. 31 people were killed almost immediately and tens of thousands of others are expected to fall victim to cancers caused

> **'Nobody in the world before has ever been confronted with an accident of this kind.'**
> *Yevgeny Velikhov, Chief Scientist, Chernobyl*

by the cloud of radioactive debris which then spread over most of Europe. The devastating spread of the Chernobyl radiation cloud showed starkly that nuclear accidents have no respect for international boundaries. One country's disaster will kill thousands in far-off nations, scientists now realize. But what was the cause?

Soviet scientists quickly established a basic sequence of events. During a break for maintenance work, reactor number 4 suddenly produced a burst of power. As a result, uranium fuel rapidly heated, overcoming the reactor's water coolant, which was turned into steam. At this high temperature the steam reacted with the element zirconium covering the fuel rods to produce hydrogen, which then ignited and exploded, blasting the reactor's lid into the air and setting fire to its graphite core. Many Western experts blamed the Chernobyl reactor's graphite core and water coolant. At high temperatures, steam and graphite react, they pointed out.

It could have been worse But according to the official Soviet report of the accident, the disaster was caused by 'procedural violations' by operators who were carrying out tests on the reactor during its maintenance closedown. Their experiment began to go wrong. They then flouted more and more safety procedures in a bid to keep their experiment going. They even switched off the reactor's emergency core-cooling system. Had it not been for the extraordinary heroism of local firemen the consequences of the explosion could have been even more appalling.

As it is, workers and soldiers took several months to plug the last vestige of escaping radiation. Today, Chernobyl reactor number 4 stands entombed in solid concrete in which it must remain for decades – a monument to the vulnerability of nuclear plants.

The core of a Soviet nuclear plant – the heart and most delicate part of its atomic furnace.

An acceptable

On 2 December 1942, a group of scientists completed construction of a strange edifice inside an old squash court at Chicago University. Built with six tonnes of uranium, 50 tonnes of uranium oxide, and 400 tonnes of graphite, it was to be the world's first nuclear reactor.

> 'The nuclear option is the cheapest, the safest and the least environmentally harmful of any existing source of electricity generation.' *Lord Sherfield, scientist*

At 2.20 p.m., the researchers' leader, Enrico Fermi, carefully removed the reactor's neutron-absorbing control rods, and initiated the first self-sustaining fission chain-reaction in history. The atomic age had begun – and within three years, led to the manufacture and detonation of the first atom bombs.

A good record? Since then more than 140 nuclear power stations have been built across the globe and these now supply a sizeable proportion of the world's energy. And although there have been some close calls, there have been no disastrous accidents and no core meltdowns.

'On its record to date, the nuclear industry has been the safest of all,' states Lord Sherfield, British scientist and politician. 'In contrast there have been in recent memory two frightful disasters to chemical plants (at Flixborough and Seveso), several mining disasters, a large number of railway accidents, and some hair-raising air crashes.'

Why then should everyone worry so much

risk?

about nuclear power, ask supporters. Because we have been very lucky so far, answer opponents: 'Fission energy is safe only if a number of critical devices work as they should; if a number of people in key positions follow all their instructions; if there is no sabotage, no hijacking of transports; if no reactor, fuel reprocessing plant or repository is situated in a region of riots or guerrilla activity, and no revolution or war takes place there,' Hannes Alfven, Nobel Prize winner, has warned.

Weighing the risk Clearly nuclear energy can never be totally safe – but then no activity is totally safe. Getting out of bed or walking down the street has its risks. In fact many say that these are greater than those attached to living near a nuclear reactor.

In one report, Professor Bernard Cohen estimates that if all America were to derive its power from nuclear reactors, and allowing for some fatal accidents, 'living next to a nuclear plant would reduce life expectancy by only 0.03 years, which makes it 150 times safer than living in a city'.

In future, improvements to present reactor designs, the introduction of more automatic and robot equipment for refuelling and handling waste, and a better understanding of radiation should further reduce the risks. But many fear this may still not be enough.

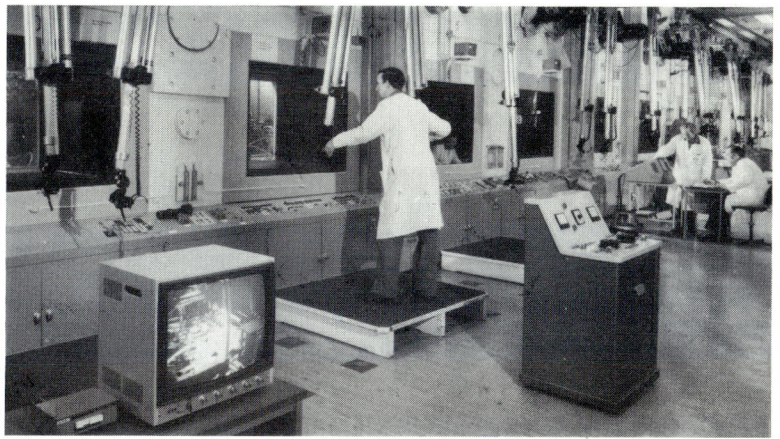

Operating a nuclear plant. These manipulator arms are used to cut down the risk of radiation.

'We don't need nuclear power. The technology is untested, the process is frightening, and the cost huge and hidden.'
H. Bacon and J. Valentine, in Power Corrupts

The aftermath of the blast at the Flixborough chemical works in 1974 which killed 28 people. No comparable disaster has ever occurred at a nuclear plant.

How safe

Inside a reactor, nuclear fuel undergoes remarkable changes. Its uranium breaks down, and apart from releasing neutrons and energy, it turns into many different elements including strontium, caesium and krypton.

> **'If the Romans had developed nuclear power, we would still be guarding their radioactive waste.'**
>
> *Friends of the Earth*

Dealing with this spent fuel – which has to be removed when a reactor is refuelled – is one of the trickiest and most controversial aspects of the nuclear industry. For one thing, the spent fuel is extremely radioactive. But it also contains valuable materials such as plutonium which can be used again as fuel.

Reprocessing Nuclear engineers have to find ways to extract that valuable fuel without risk. This is not easy and can only be carried out at special chemical complexes – known as reprocessing plants – like the one at Windscale (Sellafield) in Cumbria.

Environmentalists view these reprocessing plants with great suspicion and allege they are dangerous sources of deadly pollution. Indeed, the environmental group Friends of the Earth claims that the reprocessing of nuclear fuel 'is probably the most hazardous of all nuclear activities'.

Different wastes, different risks? Before looking more closely at these claims, it is worth discussing the make-up of nuclear waste in a little more detail. In fact, there are three different types of waste: high-, medium- and low-level, each graded according to its radioactivity.

Low-level waste includes contaminated clothing and equipment, while medium waste is similar, although slightly more radioactive. Low-level waste is generally packed in drums and buried in shallow trenches or dumped at sea.

This latter practice – even though it in-

Reactor waste encased in concrete blocks. No site has yet been picked for its disposal.

is nuclear waste?

volves relatively weak radioactive waste – is highly controversial and has been denounced at international meetings, including some organized by the United Nations.

Many countries – most recently Belgium

> 'The high level liquid waste from the entire British nuclear programme is equivalent in volume to two average sized detached houses.'
>
> *Lord Sherfield, scientist*

and Switzerland – have abandoned the practice. Others, such as Britain, have attempted to continue but have been blocked by action by transport union workers. 'We seem to have left ourselves with two choices – either we destroy this planet by pressing a button (starting a nuclear war) or we get slowly poisoned to death by dumping nuclear waste in the sea,' said James Slater of the National Union of Seamen, which banned nuclear waste dumping in 1983.

At present, medium waste is stored at nuclear plants, but one day may be buried underground.

However, the most controversial type of waste is undoubtedly the high-level variety (although a great deal of public confusion exists about the different types). This is made up of extremely radioactive materials, some with half-lives of several thousand years. (The 'half-life' of a radioactive substance is the time a lump takes to decay to a piece only half as big. For instance, one kilogram of plutonium will decay to a half-kilogram piece in 24,000 years.)

Dealing with high-level waste has caused the nuclear industry many headaches. At present, tanks of it – left over after the uranium and plutonium have been removed from spent fuel – are carefully stored above ground and must be monitored, and closely supervised, at all times. Nuclear industrialists think this is acceptable for the moment, but admit that a safer, permanent solution will be needed very soon.

Below right Nuclear waste being loaded on to a ship for burial at sea.

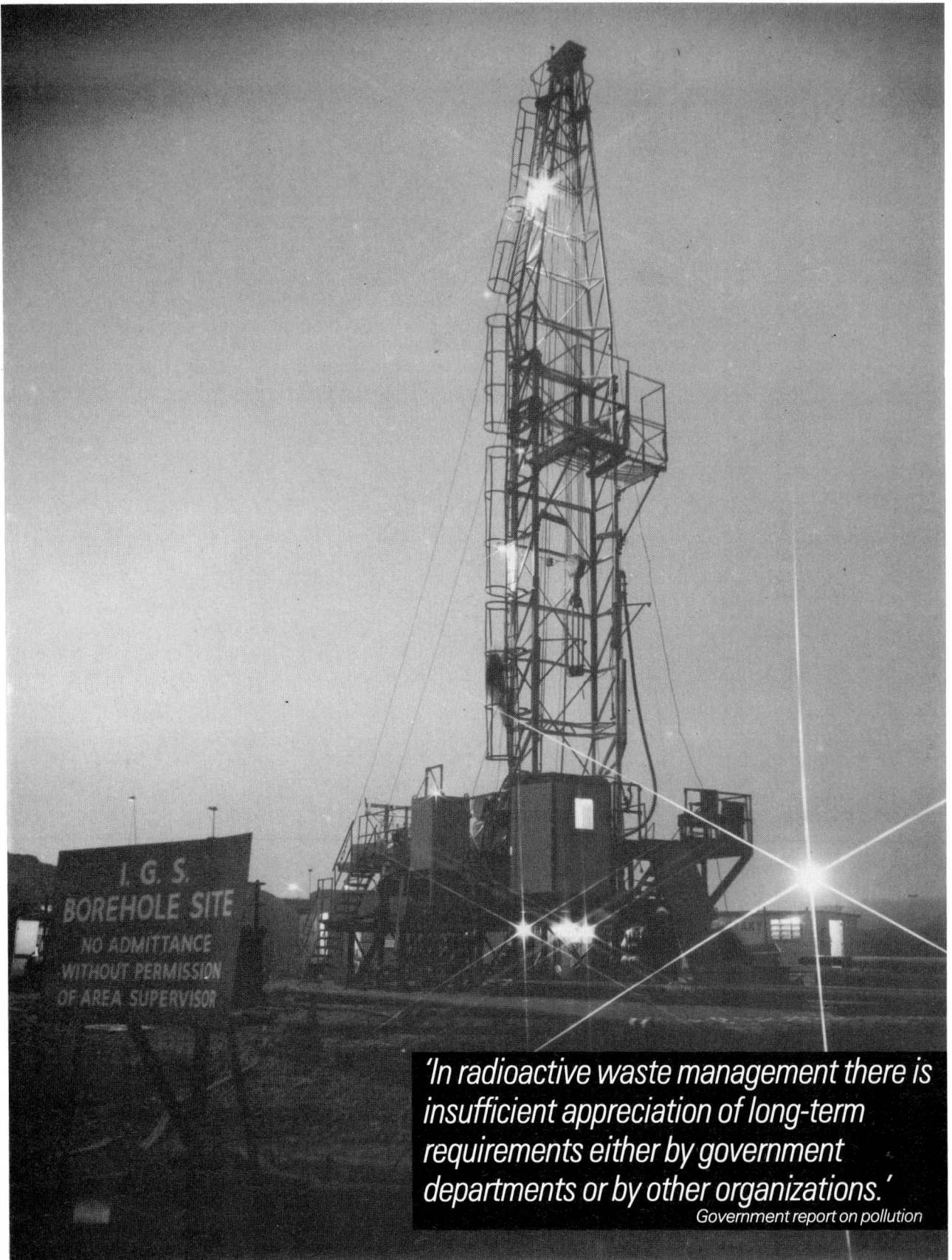

I. G. S.
BOREHOLE SITE
NO ADMITTANCE
WITHOUT PERMISSION
OF AREA SUPERVISOR

'In radioactive waste management there is insufficient appreciation of long-term requirements either by government departments or by other organizations.'
Government report on pollution

Storing up problems?

Deep below the ground, scientists and engineers one day hope to find homes for their most dangerous radioactive wastes – by burying them in special caverns a kilometre or more underground.

It sounds safe enough – but many worrying questions have been asked about possible escapes of radioactivity, and resulting

> 'The proposed method for the final storage of high-level waste is deemed to be absolutely safe.' *Swedish report*

contaminations of the countryside and of drinking water supplies. After all, say nuclear opponents, that waste will be highly radioactive for thousands of years to come – a time scale that transcends human experience.

Every possible precaution? The nuclear industry believes its nuclear waste plans will create no serious risks. The waste will first be kept above ground for many years to allow the most intense radioactivity to die down. Then it will be solidified into a glasslike substance (a process called vitrification), covered with corrosion-resistant materials and buried in sealed vaults drilled into rock seams in geologically stable areas.

There, they say, the waste should be safe. Indeed, it is believed that in many areas the natural radioactivity of rock itself will generate 'as much radioactive energy as would come from the waste products of three or four large nuclear power plants'.

How safe is safe? Such assurances give environmentalists little comfort. They warn that earth tremors might crack open containers, that diverted underground rivers could sweep radioactivity into populated areas, or that terrorists may break into the caverns and bring the waste to the surface. They also allege that insufficient research has been carried out into waste disposal, especially compared with the large sums spent on building nuclear reactors.

This point is backed, to some extent, by the report of a commission on environmental pollution chaired by Lord Flowers: 'We think that quite inadequate attention has been given to the matter (of nuclear waste disposal), and we find this more surprising in view of the large nuclear programmes that are envisaged for the coming decades.'

But nuclear proponents deny there are problems. For contamination to occur, they say, their carefully selected geological seams would have to change from being dry to wet; the corrosion-resistant waste covers would have to be penetrated; and the glass around the waste would have to be attacked and sufficiently worn through to release significant amounts of radioactive materials. This last action would take a very long time – for it is estimated that even warm water would take about a century to dissolve a millimetre of the surface of the glass – and the glass is several metres thick.

'Plain commonsense shows that the chance of any substances in the glass getting past all these barriers, in significant amounts, and in time still to be seriously radioactive when they finally emerge, must be extraordinarily small,' says one expert.

This is seen as complacent by opponents. 'Massive quantities of radioactive wastes are being, and will be produced in the future,' warned Dr Helen Caldicott, president of the US group of doctors, Physicians for Social Responsibility. 'The safe storage of waste is unsolved, and even if there were a present-day solution, we could not predict a stable society or world for half a million years. We could not guarantee incorruptible guards or moral politicians and we certainly cannot prevent earthquakes, cyclones or even wars.'

A drilling rig probes the rock strata in a bid to find a safe disposal site for radioactive waste.

Dangerous

O

On 1 November 1979, three men walked up to a goods train standing at platform 9, Stratford Station, London and pointed a rocket launcher at it. A devastating attack seemed imminent.

Fortunately, their launcher turned out to be a model. Neverthless the men's intent was serious. They were trying to publicise the dangers they associated with the transportation of nuclear waste through built up areas.

'During almost 30 years of nuclear transport, no accidents involving the release of radioactivity have ever taken place.' *British Nuclear Fuels*

Their 'target', it turned out, was a rail wagon carrying spent nuclear fuel. Many people fear that a terrorist attack or serious fire involving one of these could lead to widespread destruction and death.

Indeed, environmentalists claim that nuclear waste transport is 'the jugular vein of the nuclear power programme', that puts thousands of people at risk every day.

What happens? In Britain, most nuclear waste is carried from reactors to the country's Windscale (or Sellafield) reprocessing plant by train. In other countries, such as the United States, this task is carried out using lorries. Either way, many journeys are made, frequently through populated areas.

This waste is highly radioactive but has to be moved from reactors to processing plants so its valuable plutonium by-products can be removed. This leads to widespread transport movements – in Britain alone there are 500 a year, with more than 100 passing through London.

A remote risk? 'The release of the contents of one of these shipments would paralyze the capital for a century,' ecologists Hilary Bacon and John Valentine have warned. Already there have been twelve derailments involving nuclear waste trains. One day there may be a collision, perhaps with a chemicals train that could start a blaze which might release deadly clouds of radioactive materials. It is also possible that terrorists might attack a train and split open the waste containers with bombs.

The nuclear industry claims such risks are remote. For instance, they point out that nuclear waste has been carried by train for 30 years without a single significant accident. 'Our containers have been designed to take a great deal of serious damage – even in the worst accident,' said an official at the Central Electricity Generating Board, which is responsible for nuclear waste transport in Britain. 'We have dropped them 10 metres on to steel plated concrete, and engulfed them in an 800 deg C fire and they still have not leaked.'

As for terrorist attacks – why should they bother, ask nuclear supporters? The containers are so difficult to break open that there must be many other, easier targets for their attacks, such as road and rail containers that carry hazardous chemicals.

cargo?

'A lot of people think nuclear power has nothing to do with them. Then we point out that loads of radioactive waste are being carried past their doors. It concentrates their minds wonderfully.' *Anti-nuclear campaigner*

A nuclear waste train near Cherbourg in France – a target for angry demonstrators.

Building the Wylfa nuclear plant in Wales, 1967. It was then the biggest reactor in the world and the scale of its construction shows how complex and expensive nuclear plants had become.

cheap fuel?

When Allied forces dropped atom bombs that destroyed the Japanese cities of Hiroshima and Nagasaki in 1945, a stunned world suddenly became aware of a force that seemed to have unlimited potential. Surely, thought politicians, every nation would one day be able to tap that power and use it to solve their energy problems.

Utopian dreams? Such optimism was understandable. After all, the energy contained in a single kilo lump of uranium, when burned in a nuclear reactor, releases energy equivalent to that provided by the burning of 3,000 tonnes of coal in a conventional power plant.

Realizing this, confident scientists and politicians quickly began to make grandiose claims about the future of nuclear power. They envisaged constructing whole groups of nuclear reactors which would supply nations with all their power and for only negligible costs. Early publicity even claimed that nuclear electricity would be too cheap even to monitor.

'The day is gone when nations will fight for oil,' claimed the prize-winning author David Deitz in his 1945 book, *Atomic Energy in the Coming Era*. He was backed a year later by a leading US lawyer, James Newman, who helped draft the country's Atomic Energy Act in 1946. 'This new force offers enormous possibilities for improving public welfare, for revamping our industrial methods, and for increasing the standard of living,' he said.

Soaring costs Sadly, however, nuclear energy has not proved to be that easy to exploit. While reactors indeed use fuel that is very cheap, building a nuclear power station is anything but cheap. Installing the extremely complex safety and emergency equipment required has sent construction costs spiralling.

Costly methods had to be found to contain radiation, to provide emergency cooling in case of accidents, to monitor automatically the highly radioactive cores, to refuel the reactor while it was still in operation, and to build the giant concrete and steel domes over the reactor to hold in any serious fuel and waste leaks.

As a result, construction costs soared far above those of traditional power plants and the price of electricity from nuclear power has remained at about the same level as that provided by traditional generating plants.

Increasingly, engineers have chosen to build very large nuclear power plants to make them most economical. Unfortunately, this can lead to astronomical leaps in costs when design errors have been made.

> 'The capital cost of a nuclear power station, if spent instead on energy saving, would save three times more energy than the station would produce in its lifetime.'
> Sir Martin Ryle, Astronomer Royal

Too much

Around the world, governments have found themselves confronted with massive leaps in costs for the reactors they had earlier planned in the rush of enthusiasm for nuclear energy.

'Cost overruns on nuclear projects have become endemic and devastating', states Christopher Flavin, in the Worldwide Institute report, *Nuclear Power, the Market Test*. 'In the past ten years, nuclear construction costs have risen 60 per cent in France, more than doubled in West Germany and more than trebled in the United States.'

In America alone, one Department of Energy study of 47 nuclear plants found that 36 of these cost at least twice their initial, estimated price, while 13 of them were four times higher.

Other examples are even more alarming. A giant 1,100 megawatt reactor at Shoreham, Long Island, was originally expected to cost £160 million. A decade behind schedule, it is now thought the reactor will cost £2,670 million. As a result, its backers, the Long Island Lighting Company, have had to pay more than £660,000 a day in interest on money they had borrowed to build the plant.

And in Britain, an entire series – the advanced gas-cooled reactors (AGRs) – were blighted by cost and construction problems.

The story of the AGR Built to replace Britain's first generation of Magnox nuclear plants, these reactors were designed in the 1960s to have improved energy production. Each was planned to provide around 600 million watts of electricity – enough to power 600,000 small electric fires.

In a burst of nuclear enthusiasm, the government of the day ordered five giant twin-reactor stations – although its scientists' previous experience had been limited to building only one small test AGR. 'We have hit the jackpot this time,' claimed the Minister for Power, Mr Fred Lee.

These proved to be rash words, for in the rush to build the reactors, three different consortia of companies were set up to build three different types of AGR – a move which many believe spread the nation's nuclear expertise too thinly.

On top of this, industrial disputes, management rows and design changes during construction began to plague the AGR. Long delays set in and by the 1980s only two reactors – at Hunterston and Hinkley Point – had been built. Of the rest, only one of each planned pair of reactors had been built and these have suffered frequent operating problems.

Prices also spiralled alarmingly. For instance, the construction of one AGR – at

Opposite The Heysham B reactor – one of Britain's advanced gas-cooled reactors whose construction costs have soared to 'catastrophic' levels.

34

too soon?

Dungeness – was expected finally to cost more than six times its original estimate of £89 million. As one glum electricity chief later stated: 'The AGR is a catastrophe we must never repeat.'

Has the lesson been learnt? All these examples make dispiriting reading, and suggest that nuclear power has little to offer the future. However, nuclear industry chiefs now say they have stopped these massive rises in costs and have licked their design and construction problems. Opponents say they see no sign of this and claim that the costs will continue to soar and the problems to multiply.

'The first lesson we've learned is "Don't build nuclear plants in America".'
Don Beeth, Houston Lighting and Power Company

'The case for nuclear power is unassailable.'
Nigel Lawson, former UK energy secretary

The world is using more and more energy. In only the past 30 years, energy consumption has trebled. Yet, strangely, the world's sources of energy have hardly altered for centuries. Despite new technologies, and nuclear power, three-quarters of our energy is still supplied by fossil fuels.

> 'The end of coal was reliably predicted before the end of the 19th century. Today there appears to be more recoverable coal than ever.' *Colin Sweet, Centre for Energy Studies*

Both coal and oil are fossil fuels. Coal is the fossilized remains of primeval vegetation, oil is the fossilized remains of tiny sea creatures. These living beings survived because they could absorb the warmth of sunlight. When we burn coal and oil we are releasing that sunlight, which has been stored below ground for millions of years. Needless to say, there is no way we can replace that energy at the rate we are using it up.

King Coal Coal was used more than 2,000 years ago. Roman soldiers even burned it on their tours of duty in the cold north. Later, during the 16th century, it became increasingly important, replacing wood – as most European forests had been chopped down by then – as a fuel for brewing, smelting and many other industries.

Later new technologies were developed to improve coal mining – including the construction of the first steam engines which were used to pump water out of mines and to raise coal to the surface.

Coal powered the Industrial Revolution

Coal – used by man for 2,000 years and still an important energy source.

Fossil fuels

and was used to run mills and factories, ships and railways. By 1880, more than 140 million tonnes of coal were burned in Britain each year and it remains an important source of energy. Nowadays Britain uses about 120 million tonnes, while the United States uses about 540 million, Russia 450 million and West Germany 100 million tonnes.

Black gold Oil has had a more recent leap to fame. It was hardly used 100 years ago. Now it provides 38 per cent of the world's energy.

There are several reasons for oil's relatively sudden popularity – because it is a liquid it can be easily moved about in tankers or pipelines, and it is the best fuel discovered so far for cars and aircraft. Crude oil is also extremely versatile and can be refined into plastics, tars, lubricants and a multitude of other products.

Natural gas This is another fossil fuel which is often found together with oil. When burned, it can be a useful source of heat. In the immediate future it is likely that natural gas will be a valuable form of power, but like oil, it will probably run out in a relatively short time.

The future of fossil fuels? Fossil fuels have been with us for a long time, but scientists are still working hard to improve their use. Some are trying to find better ways to get more oil out of existing wells, others are trying to find a replacement for oil when it runs out, by making synthetic, oil-like liquid fuels out of coal which could be pumped through pipes and used to run cars, planes and ships. Unfortunately, such research is proving expensive and difficult. And problems of depletion are not the only drawback to using fossil fuels.

Oil – now so valuable that expensive technology, such as this production platform, has been developed to pump it from below the seabed.

'Man-made emissions of greenhouse gases promise to impose a warming of unusual dimensions on a global climate that is already unusually warm.' US National Academy of Sciences

Fossil fuel dangers

Like a blanket that keeps a sleeper warm, carbon dioxide in our atmosphere absorbs and holds heat. And every year we pump more and more carbon dioxide into the air by burning fossil fuels, such as coal and oil, which contain carbon. One day it is feared we may pump out so much that the earth could become dangerously hot. Glaciers and ice fields would melt, low-lying countries would be flooded, and the world's climate would be utterly changed.

> 'Temperature increases are likely to be accompanied by dramatic changes in precipitation and a rise in global sea level.'
>
> US Environmental Protection Agency

That sounds like a scene from a science fiction disaster movie – but many scientists are now worried that it could come true. There is evidence that carbon dioxide levels in the air have risen by more than 40 per cent in the past 100 years – because of industrialization and increased coal- and oil-burning.

The greenhouse effect Every hour more than 500,000 tonnes of carbon are burned around the world by car engines and factories, and are pumped into the air as carbon dioxide. As a result, the atmosphere is likely to retain more and more of the heat we get from sunlight, instead of radiating it back into outer space. This is called the 'greenhouse effect' – for that is how greenhouses keep plants warm. One day the entire planet could become as hot as a greenhouse.

Already, the Environmental Protection Agency of the United States government has issued its own stark warning – that global temperatures could rise by up to 6 deg C next century, enough to cause widespread havoc. Weather patterns around the world would be completely altered; rainfall patterns would change; rivers would swell or dry up; and with the melting of the ice caps the level of the seas would rise dramatically. Indeed 'we may get into trouble in ways we have barely imagined', warned the US National Academy of Sciences.

Other scientists have been more cautious, suggesting that temperatures may not rise that rapidly because the oceans will absorb much of the extra heat. Nevertheless, there is broad agreement that the greenhouse effect will soon become a serious problem.

Acid rain Unfortunately, fossil fuels have other unwelcome side effects. Factories which burn coal and oil produce acidic oxides of sulphur and nitrogen. These gases dissolve in the clouds and later fall to the ground as acid rain.

Already there have been reports that acid rain has killed all aquatic life in hundreds of lakes and rivers in Canada, Sweden and America; released lead from water pipes; damaged soil and eroded buildings; stunted forests; and increased respiratory illnesses.

Many of these claims still have to be investigated, but it is clear that the problem is growing. The difficulty for governments trying to control acid rain is that the factories responsible for it are often not in the same country. Sweden, for instance, blames Britain for the acid rain which falls on its lakes. Trying to resolve questions of responsibility in such circumstances can take a long time.

No easy answer? It would seem that even standard 'safe' fuels, like oil and coal, have unpleasant side-effects and, like nuclear fuel, can be regarded as potential threats to the environment. Only renewable energy sources, that tap the power of the sun, wind and tides, are both safe and will not run out. But they too present problems.

Renewable

Each year, every human being, on average, uses energy equivalent to the burning of approximately 3 tonnes of coal. This power is used for heat, transport and electricity. At the moment it comes from the world's three principal energy sources – oil, coal and uranium, but reserves of these are quickly running out.

Some politicians and scientists believe the only answer is to build more nuclear reactors. Others want to exploit renewable energy sources that cannot run out and do not pose any threats to the environment. These include the sun, wind and tides.

Solar power Of these, solar power has perhaps the greatest potential – for, every day, energy from the sun pours down on our planet. Indeed as much solar energy falls on the earth in an hour as all the world's nations consume as fuel in a whole year. It is a remarkable free gift, and is likely to last for ever. Unfortunately its exploitation is no straightforward matter.

One problem is that, although plentiful, sunlight does not actually make things very hot. It is used in some countries – such as Israel – to heat water for homes, but generating electricity requires a temperature of several hundred degrees. To reach this, sunlight must be concentrated in some way – usually by using very large mirrors. These can only operate in direct sunlight and must be moved as the sun itself moves across the sky – a tricky procedure that also uses up energy.

One answer may be to build solar ray collectors in space and then beam their power to the ground. Such assemblies are possible but would require costly and difficult construction, and are unlikely to become practical undertakings this century.

Wind power For more than 1,000 years, mankind has been exploiting the energy of the winds. Indeed, until the last century, wind was a major source of power, harnessed by windmills that milled, ground and pumped, as well as by sailing ships.

But these machines were relatively inefficient, and were replaced by steam engines and later by diesel and electric motors. However, some scientists now believe that modern technology can help design improved windmills able to convert wind energy into electricity. Already, many countries have designed prototype wind generators – giant groups of rotor blades mounted on towers to catch gusts that can travel at up to 120 kph. To survive such conditions, the rotor blades must be very strong, but they must also be light so they can revolve easily. Finding the right materials for the blades is a major problem in building wind generators.

At the moment, scientists do not believe that wind generators can provide much more than 500 kilowatts of power, enough for a very small town. To produce larger amounts, many hundreds of giant towers would have to be built, causing major disruptions to the countryside.

Wave power Every day, the world's coasts are battered by waves of enormous power.

Right Wind power – vertical axis turbines at Albuquerque in New Mexico. Modern technology is helping to improve the design of machines that tap one of the world's most ancient energy sources.

energy

Surely, say researchers, we can harness that incredible energy and use it to generate electricity. Indeed, they point out that in deep seas, a one-metre section of a wave front can carry 100 kilowatts of power.

The trouble is that – like wind generators – wave machines must be made of very strong materials to survive their hostile environment. But they must also be light so that their individual parts can move easily and turn the turbines.

'If a wave converter is to survive constant battering – in the North Atlantic it would encounter between two and three million waves each year – it must be massively built. Yet if it is over-engineered it will be expensive and unable to compete with other sources of energy,' points out Dr Michael Flood of Friends of the Earth.

As yet, scientists have not managed to balance these different demands but still insist that wave power, and solar and wind power, have enormous potential. As designs are continually improved they should at least reduce our dependence on present traditional energy sources.

Sunny side up? Solar reflectors can be used as cookers, as here in Geneva, but they need warm sunshine.

Geothermal power

D eep below the surface of the earth, rocks are heated to temperatures that would melt metals. Sometimes – in countries where there are volcanoes or geological instability

– this happens quite near the surface. Then underground streams and pools are boiled off into steam, coming to the surface as hot springs and geysers. These can then be exploited to make power. In New Zealand, natural hot water is used to generate 10 per cent of the country's electricity. In Iceland, it is piped off to heat homes directly.

Artificial geysers Since few countries have natural sources of heat which bubble so conveniently from the ground, scientists are now trying to build artificial ones by drilling miles down into the ground.

Test centres have already been built – including ones in New Mexico, and in Cornwall, England. There engineers have drilled parallel wells 2 km deep, and at the very bottom have set off explosions to create an intricate web of fissures which join the two wells. By pumping cold water down one well, forcing it through the network of fissures and bringing it hot to the surface, a new source of energy can be exploited.

Geothermal stations would use the hot, pressurized water to drive turbines and generate electricity, and would have several advantages. They would tap a virtually inexhaustible power source – the earth – and could be used almost anywhere in the world. 'Geothermal energy has fewer risks associated with it than any other form of power generation and has the advantage of great flexibility of operation,' says Dr Tony Batchelor, director of the geothermal research group at the Camborne School of Mines.

But there are drawbacks as well. Even at very great depths, 6 km underground, rocks – which get their heat from the earth's core – can only warm water to about 200 deg C. Turbines are fairly inefficient when used at these relatively low temperatures. Drilling the deep wells is also very difficult – and expensive.

Does it have a future? At present scientists agree that geothermal electricity would cost two or three times that produced by normal means. However, in remote areas or on islands, where power transmission is costly, it may prove useful. The excess hot water could even be used to heat homes and greenhouses.

Meanwhile scientists are working on ways to improve drilling and generating equipment, and may make enough progress one day to allow wider exploitation of the power that lies beneath our feet.

The heat below our feet – underground hot water is pumped from a well below Paris and is used to heat these apartment blocks at Villeneuve la Garenne.

Is fusion

The doughnut-shaped interior of the JET reactor vessel at Culham. One day scientists hope to use it to recreate the power that has kept the sun burning for billions of years.

the future?

For billions of years, the sun has burned steadily in the sky, providing the earth with life-giving heat and light. The source of this mighty power is nuclear fusion – where hydrogen atoms coalesce to form helium, and in the process release vast amounts of energy. Many believe that if scientists could harness nuclear fusion it would be the answer to all our energy problems.

Chasing a dream? That goal has proved to be remarkably elusive. For the past 30 years, scientists around the world have spent billions of dollars, pounds and roubles on fusion research – without success. The closest they have come to harnessing fusion is to make hydrogen bombs. Indeed, their search has been likened to a hunt for a lost gold mine by one expert, Professor Lidsky of the Massachusetts Institute of Technology. 'Only a few believers are absolutely certain that the goal exists,' he says, 'but the search takes place over interesting ground and the rewards for success are overwhelming.'

This is no understatement. Less than half a cubic mile of seawater would provide enough deuterium – an isotope of hydrogen – to power fusion reactors which could then produce as much energy as the world's entire present oil reserves.

Why hasn't it happened? Designing fusion reactors is a very tricky undertaking. The hydrogen atoms have to be heated to extremely high temperatures, about 100 million deg C, before they will fuse into helium. At these temperatures, the gases would vapourize the reactor walls, so scientists have had to use powerful magnetic fields to contain them. Unfortunately, no way has yet been found to stop these from leaking.

> **'Fusion power is one of the most promising of all energy sources for the future.'**
> UK Atomic Energy Authority

The best system, called a Tokamak, is Russian, and holds the hydrogen in a large doughnut-shaped magnetic container. A giant Tokamak has just been built by an EEC consortium at Culham, England, and scientists hope to use it to learn finally how to generate power from nuclear fusion. It may take a decade before they are ready to build a demonstration power plant. If successful, the world will then get its first fusion reactors – but not before the year 2020, at the earliest!

Even then, fusion power will have drawbacks: it is not a completely cheap, limitless, safe energy source as is sometimes claimed. By the time it is ready for widespread use, several hundred billion pounds will have been spent on its development. It will require supplies of lithium for its operation, and these are limited. It will also emit slight amounts of radiation which will have to be contained.

Scientists have also begun working on other ways to control fusion – by blasting hydrogen with lasers, for instance. At the moment though, research on these laser devices is well behind research into Tokamaks. It seems clear that whatever system we pick, we will still have a long wait before fusion power is with us on a large scale.

Fast breeders –

Uranium – like coal and oil – is a limited resource. One day, but not for several hundred years, we will have used it all up if we continue to burn it at present rates. And if we expand the nuclear industry, as many wish, we will use it up even faster.

It sounds an important drawback – but nuclear scientists have come up with a solution. They have developed a reactor that makes more fuel than it burns. This remarkable machine is called a fast breeder reactor – and without it, long-term plans for nuclear power are impossible.

However, fast breeder reactors are also highly controversial. They operate at very high temperatures (about 290 deg C) and are tricky to build and control. They also produce large quantities of plutonium, and many people fear this could be used to make nuclear bombs.

How fast breeders work As discussed on page 13, only one type of uranium – uranium 235 – supports a chain reaction and can make heat. But the other type – uranium 238 – still undergoes a change if it is struck by a neutron. It turns into plutonium. Plutonium can also be used as a fuel. Normal reactors only

The world's first fast breeder reactor that generated electricity – the Dounreay plant on the north coast of Scotland.

are they safe?

burn uranium, but fast breeder reactors burn plutonium, while also producing excess amounts of it!

To achieve this, many more neutrons are required, so all parts of the reactor's core which might absorb them are removed, and the amount of coolant is reduced. A blanket of uranium 238 is wrapped round the core and some of this is slowly transformed into plutonium as the reactor operates.

Should more be built? Already several fast breeder reactors have been built – at Dounreay in Scotland, at Creys-Malville in France, and in Idaho, in the United States. Russia has also constructed fast breeders.

Supporters claim these building programmes should be stepped up to free the world of the risk of uranium running out. 'Breeder reactors will be needed in large numbers in the twenty-first century and their development therefore constitutes an essential option in our energy strategy,' stated F. L. Tombs, chairman of the Electricity Council.

Opponents of nuclear energy, however, consider fast breeders a particularly dangerous type of reactor. Because they operate at such intense heats, if accidents did occur, they would more rapidly heat to dangerous levels than standard reactors. If ordinary reactors aren't safe, then fast breeders are ten times less safe, they say.

Fast breeders would also produce large amounts of plutonium, which could cause problems. 'To operate a network of fast breeder reactors it would be necessary to separate, process and transport large quantities of plutonium about the country,' Friends of the Earth state. 'Therein lies a daunting security problem.'

They and other opponents point out that, if many fast breeder reactors are built, the world would either have to use up this plutonium in normal reactors, or find means of storing it. Either way, we should have entered a new plutonium age.

The fast breeder – which uses sodium to remove the intense heat which its core produces.

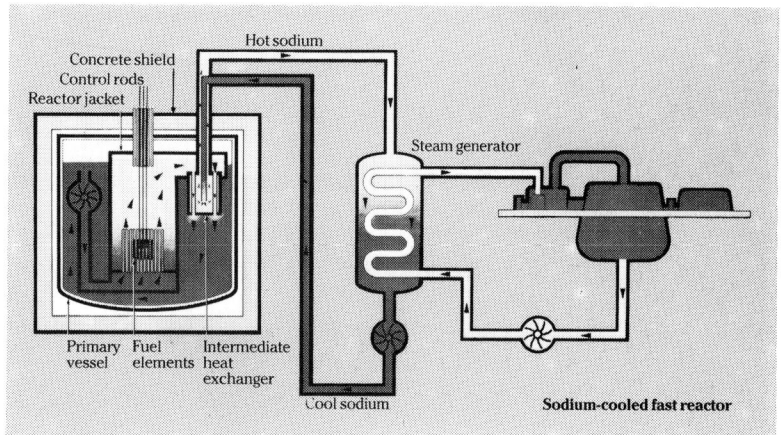

Hot sodium

Concrete shield
Control rods
Reactor jacket

Steam generator

Primary vessel   Fuel elements   Intermediate heat exchanger

Cool sodium

Sodium-cooled fast reactor

'The fast breeder reactor will be the most obvious source of energy in 25 years' time.'
Sir John Hill, UK Atomic Energy Authority, 1977

A plutonium

'A major commitment to fission power and
the plutonium economy should be
postponed as long as possible because of its
grave potential implications to mankind.'

Government report, 1976

A nuclear plant at Dodewaard
in Holland – surrounded by
fences and barbed wire that
would do credit to a
concentration camp.

economy?

A plutonium economy – in which the world's power generation would increasingly depend on a particularly dangerous and highly radioactive element – is generally viewed with apprehension and fear.

But plutonium has been with the world for more than 40 years. It is – as we have mentioned – a common by-product of all nuclear reactors. Why should there be so much fuss about fast breeder reactors then? After all, we seem to have survived a plutonium economy quite well so far.

A threat to civil liberties? Opponents believe that the more plutonium there is, the greater is the risk of some being stolen to make nuclear bombs. They also fear that, in order to prevent such thefts, governments would take such repressive measures that civil liberties would be curtailed.

This claim is vividly illustrated in a statement made by former British energy secretary Anthony Wedgwood Benn, an early supporter of nuclear power and now an opponent. 'You have to protect plutonium with absolute maximum security,' he warned. 'Dounreay (site of Britain's fast breeder reactor) was once a lovely research centre with pipe-smoking professors. Now it is an army camp with barbed wire, guard dogs, arc lights and an armed constabulary.'

He, and many others, fear that the civil authorities will have to take increasingly severe measures to protect their growing stocks of plutonium. In the end, all discussion of nuclear issues would be suppressed, with suspect groups and individuals under close state surveillance.

Another opponent, David Widdicombe, a lawyer, has said: 'A large and increasing part of our electricity would be produced under quasi-military conditions, conducted by independent corporations largely beyond democratic control.'

Misplaced fears? Nuclear supporters reject such claims as nonsense, and say it is quite wrong to suggest that stocks of plutonium will grow rapidly because we build fast breeder reactors. They point out that fast breeders could even easily be used to reduce world plutonium stocks. By using up plutonium as fuel – which normal reactors cannot – these reactors would use up stocks that would otherwise be potential targets for theft or attack.

Not surprisingly, this does not satisfy opponents who consider it highly unlikely that governments will ever reject the option of making such a valuable and useful fuel as plutonium. If the means is there to make it, it will surely be used, they say.

Are we building

Plutonium is renowned as one of the world's most dangerous substances. Inhaling only a few millionths of a gram is enough to cause eventual cancer, leukaemia or death. And if you were to put together a mere 10 kilograms of it (producing a lump the size of a grapefruit) you would have a bomb with the equivalent force of 100 tonnes of TNT. Set off in a city centre, by terrorists or fanatics, it would demolish several blocks of buildings.

The thought is a frightening and disturbing one – especially when we realize that power stations already manufacture several tens of thousands of kilograms of plutonium each year. A minute fraction of that, wrongly used, would be enough to cause havoc.

How simple would it be? Dr Bhupendra Jasani, of the Stockholm International Peace Research Institute, has warned: 'Making reliable fission weapons for the military is complicated, but a crude, inefficient nuclear device is not beyond the capacity of a small group of people.' Indeed, a recent report pointed out that if terrorists obtained plutonium, they would only need equipment that was 'no more elaborate than that used by criminals to manufacture heroin' to prepare an A-bomb. The task would cost a mere £10,000 and could be undertaken by only three or four people.

Others feel these fears are exaggerated. For one thing, the plutonium produced by civil reactors contains isotopes that limit its use as an A-bomb fuel. (The military use special reactors which are refuelled at great speed in order to obtain pure bomb-type plutonium.) This makes it less likely that terrorists could use the plutonium from a civil reactor to build an atom bomb, although this would not be, as was once believed, an impossible feat.

Obtaining that plutonium would also be extremely difficult for it would certainly be well guarded. 'Anyway, there are much easier ways to kill large numbers of people – such as introducing poisons into ventilation systems,' one leading US expert, Professor Bernard Cohen, has suggested.

But opponents fear that it may simply be enough for terrorists to make people believe that they have the plutonium, in order to achieve their aims.

The lost plutonium? Although power plants keep careful stock of their plutonium, tiny amounts do get lost – and these accumulate. For instance, between 1970 and 1977, a total of 96 kilograms was 'lost' through accounting errors at Britain's Windscale (Sellafield) plant. It is possible that criminals could convince the authorities that they had obtained some and so hold them to ransom.

One suggested answer is to 'spike' all plutonium with ferociously radioactive materials that would quickly kill those not properly equipped to handle them; this would remove the risk of threats, either real or bogus. However, the solution itself would be rather hazardous and would probably not deter an irrational terrorist determined to become a martyr.

The aftermath of a saboteurs' attack on a French oil depot – a more likely target for terrorism than a nuclear plant?

bomb factories?

'It is not a question of whether someone will deliberately acquire plutonium for the purposes of terrorism or blackmail, but only of when and how often.' David Widdicombe, lawyer

Can proliferation

On 7 June 1981, a squadron of Israeli jet fighters took off for Baghdad, the capital of Iraq. Once outside the city, they pinpointed the country's Tuwaitha Nuclear Research Centre and promptly destroyed its 40-megawatt reactor in a devastating bomb and rocket attack.

The raid was implemented, Israeli Prime Minister Menachem Begin later claimed, because Iraq was using the reactor to make nuclear weapons.

This allegation was furiously denied by Iraq which pointed out that it – unlike Israel – was a signatory of the Non-Proliferation Treaty which seeks to limit the spread of nuclear weapons round the world. The reactor had just been inspected – and cleared – by the International Atomic Energy Authority.

A real danger? This raid reflected a common enough fear – that the spread of nuclear power will give increasing numbers of states access to nuclear weapons.

But nuclear supporters, including the scientist Sir Fred Hoyle, reject this. 'Nothing concerning nuclear energy will prevent there being large stores of nuclear bombs in the world, for large stores already exist,' he says. 'Indeed, it seems much more likely that these already-existing bombs will actually be used if the world runs desperately short of energy, than if the world becomes energy-rich.'

It is also pointed out that nations seeking to make nuclear weapons could just as easily build uranium-enrichment plants and use the uranium 235 from these to make atom bombs.

Is it spreading? It is clear that building more and more nuclear power plants will mean that more and more people will obtain knowledge of nuclear matters. One day they might exploit that to make bombs, or could be forced to do so in a country where there has been a revolution or military takeover.

Twenty-three nations have already built nuclear plants and a further six are planning to build their own. Nuclear knowledge certainly appears to be spreading – but is it?

In fact, according to most analysts, that spread has now virtually halted. 'Since the mid-seventies the nuclear plans of developing countries have been substantially reduced,' the Worldwatch Institute reported. Frequently these nations found nuclear power too complex and technologically demanding for their needs – although that could quite easily change in coming years.

The world of atomic power

Countries with nuclear plants	Number of reactors (Twin reactors count 2)	% of country's total power
Argentina	2	10
Belgium	6	45
Brazil	1	2
Britain	17	16
Bulgaria	4	29
Canada	14	11
Czechoslovakia	3	Not known
Finland	4	40
France	32	48
Germany (East)	5	12
Germany (West)	15	17
Hungary	1	Not known
India	4	3
Italy	3	4
Japan	24	19
Netherlands	1	5
South Korea	3	13
Spain	7	9
Switzerland	4	28
Taiwan	4	40
United States	82	13
USSR	40	7
Yugoslavia	1	Not known

Countries now building their first reactors include China, the Philippines, South Africa, Poland, Rumania, and Mexico.

be controlled?

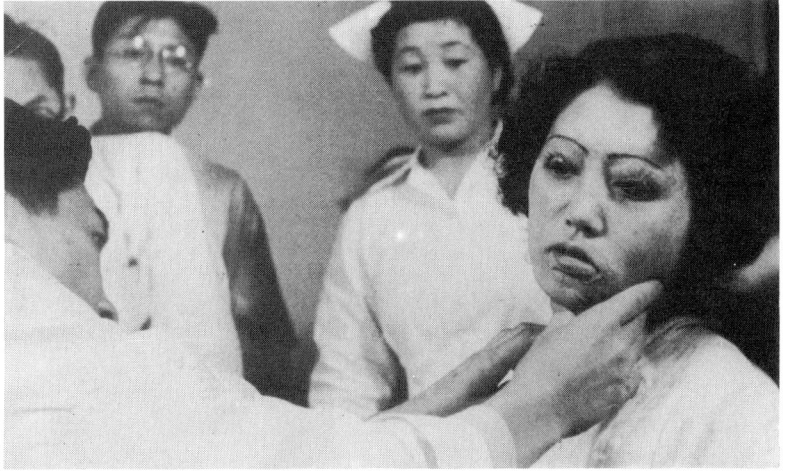

Right A victim of the atomic age – a Hiroshima survivor is examined by doctors.

Below Hiroshima – after the bomb fell. A lesson to us all?

'The greatest danger associated with nuclear power is that it provides more and more countries with access to equipment, materials and technology necessary for the manufacture of nuclear weapons.'

Friends of the Earth

MUTANT

43% HUMAN GENES
HALF-LIFE 1537 YRS

DO NOT APPROACH CLOSER THAN 17·5 METRE!

DANGER!

GOVERNMENT ISSUE PROTECTIVE SUIT Mk1

An anti-nuclear demonstrator –
one of many who now claim
that atomic power will bring
worldwide destruction.

No escape?

Nuclear power has been with us for four decades now – and never has it been more unpopular. Highly publicized accidents have led to growing opposition and, in the past ten years, many nuclear protest and environmental groups – such as Friends of the Earth, Citizens Against Nuclear Power, Greenpeace, and others – have campaigned against nuclear energy programmes.

These groups have held huge and generally peaceful rallies to publicize their campaigns in many countries including the United States, Japan, Britain, West Germany and others. But just how successful have they been? Reactor building has indeed slowed down, but this may well be because economic conditions have changed. They are just as likely to change again in the near future, resulting in new reactor programmes.

Indeed, once launched down the nuclear road, could a country ever go back if there was popular pressure to do so? It is difficult to be sure, but it seems unlikely. Nuclear knowledge is not something you can forget.

Certainly any nation that has spent many thousands of millions of pounds on developing nuclear power is unlikely to abandon it at the drop of a hat and close all reactors, unless there was a very strong reason for doing so – a disaster, for example, such as a core meltdown. Instead the most likely hope for environmentalists is that popular feeling will turn against nuclear power and that new construction programmes will be halted.

How great is the energy gap? Any decision about nuclear power also depends on future energy needs, and how quickly stocks of coal and oil run down. Any country – no matter how powerful its anti-nuclear movement – that finds itself running out of power for its factories and homes will take any energy option that comes its way – be it nuclear, solar or any other power.

And of all the choices, nuclear supporters are quite clear which is best. They believe that without nuclear power there will be anarchy as nations fight to secure dwindling energy resources. 'The development of nuclear energy is really a safeguard, probably an essential safeguard, against the outbreak of nuclear war,' claims Sir Fred Hoyle.

Opponents dispute this, of course, saying that future energy demands have been grossly exaggerated to make nuclear power look more attractive. They believe we can easily manage for three or four more decades on existing sources, combined with better conservation. By that time fusion power should be ready to meet all our energy needs.

> 'I have come to the conclusion that there is no such thing as a dispassionate viewpoint on nuclear energy.' *Civil servant*

It sounds attractive – but such a scenario is not without drawbacks. For one thing, it is not clear to what extent the continued burning of coal and oil will increase the greenhouse heating of the atmosphere, or affect the fall of acid rain. Nor is fusion power the perfect energy source – it will produce some radioactivity, and deplete exhaustible resources, such as lithium.

Big business? There is a further crucial consideration which environmentalists acknowledge – the nuclear industry itself. This has grown rapidly over the decades, fed on lucrative government contracts. As a result, the many different companies which exist in the West to build nuclear plants have grown into a powerful cartel. Faced with a lack of orders at home, they will simply look elsewhere in the world to promote reactor construction.

Indeed, in the words of one American anti-nuclear campaigner, Alvin Weinberg, nuclear power is 'a Faustian bargain that society has made with the nuclear industry'. It is a bargain that will not easily be broken.

The politics

Harnessing nuclear energy has brought countries power – power not just to keep lights burning and homes warm, but power that has provided them with political strength. It has enabled them to build atomic weapons to deter aggressors or threaten neighbours, and has also provided them with energy sources that might become invaluable when the oil runs out.

'The institutions and treaties supporting non-proliferation are in trouble.'

William Walker and Mans Lonnroth

At one time, when nuclear reactors were first built, politicians believed every country would soon have its own limitless supply of energy (and presumably political independence too). Sadly nuclear energy has not fulfilled that promise.

One problem has been the cost of developing reactors. Only rich nations have been able to afford them. On top of this, the swift growth of nuclear power in these countries led to fears that uncontrolled access throughout the world would one day lead to the widespread manufacture of nuclear bombs that would inevitably be used in time of war.

International monitoring To counter such fears, a special nuclear security group – the International Atomic Energy Authority – was set up. In 1968, under the Non-Proliferation of Nuclear Weapons Treaty, it was given special powers to inspect nuclear plants to check they are not being used to make bombs. The aim of the treaty was to curb the spread of nuclear weapons, but also to control the growth in the peaceful uses of atomic energy. More than 100 countries have signed it.

The treaty restricts nuclear weapons manufacture only to those nations who first built atomic bombs – such as Russia, Amer-

The old and the new. *Right* Chinese workers use manual effort to saw wood. *Opposite* A Western worker supervises the same task which is carried out by automated machines. Such increased efficiency is only possible through the use of electricity, which industrialized countries take for granted but the Third World cannot afford.

# of energy

ica and Britain. In return these nations agreed to supply expertise and materials to help other countries develop peaceful nuclear energy programmes.

It sounds promising. Unfortunately, the nuclear industry has proved difficult to control. The recent slump in orders for new reactors in the West has only led to increased pressure to gain orders for reactors in developing countries.

'These countries are now fighting to gain a share of a limited export market and there are bound to be growing temptations to cut corners on safeguards and technology transfer to secure orders,' state energy experts William Walker and Mans Lonnroth. They believe the United States on one hand, and France, Germany and Japan on the other, are lining up for a major international battle to sell reactors to the Third World. This would inevitably increase the risk of weapons proliferation.

The poverty trap Whether developing countries will be able to afford these reactors is another matter. Many nations in Africa and Asia are facing a cruel dilemma. They need money to build reactors so they can obtain the plentiful energy they need to build up new industries. But at present they have no energy sources of their own, and so cannot raise the first down-payments on a nuclear plant. This dilemma is only likely to get worse as traditional fuel sources dry up.

As a result some scientists and politicians have suggested that the West should hand over its last oil supplies so they can be used exclusively by the poorer nations. There seems little likelihood of this ever happening, however, so preciously is energy guarded by the West.

It is clear that the world faces many agonizing problems in dealing with the coming energy crisis, and that nuclear power alone will not solve them.

Which

Nuclear energy is a highly emotive topic and both opponents and supporters have come to adopt vociferous and extreme positions. Nevertheless, few supporters of nuclear energy would argue that it has absolutely no drawbacks. They just believe it has less than any other option.

The following is an attempt to sum up the advantages and disadvantages of nuclear energy, and also those of the world's other main energy sources.

Nuclear energy Powered by a relatively cheap fuel, which if made in fast breeder reactors, should never run out. It is capable of meeting all our electricity generation needs for the foreseeable future. However, it suffers from the danger of radiation leaks and poss-ibly of core meltdown, and there are also problems in getting rid of radioactive waste.

Oil An excellent, light, easily transportable fuel. Unfortunately supplies appear to be disappearing rapidly, perhaps within the next generation at present rates of consumption. Responsible for pollution caused by oil spills. Expensive to locate.

Coal Also a useful fuel, although less transportable than oil. Will still be in demand for some time, although there are worries about its side effects such as acid rain and the heating of the atmosphere. (Oil also produces these but not as badly.) Coal reserves will last at least 50 years. Mining costs will increase as accessible stocks get used up.

Standard sources of energy:
Right The Dounreay nuclear power station in Scotland.
Far right A rig drilling for oil off the Californian coast.

Right Coal being loaded for local distribution.
Far right A hydroelectric dam in the Elburz Mountains which supplies Tehran with much of its electricity.

energy?

Natural gas Only recently exploited. There may be another 150 years of reserves left in the world. The gas – which is mostly made up of methane – is useful for heating, but not as a car or aircraft fuel. It is also difficult to transport.

Solar energy Exploits a virtually unlimited source – the sun. Unfortunately it has proved difficult and expensive to transform into electricity, although this may improve.

Wind, tides and waves All exploit virtually unlimited day-to-day forces that should never run out. Suffer because they would use as yet unperfected, environmentally disruptive equipment that is also extremely expensive to build.

Geothermal energy Again exploits a virtually inexhaustible source, but at present is too expensive to use except in remote regions.

Conservation Not actually an energy source, but worth taking seriously. Schemes, such as combined heat-and-power programmes, which use waste heat from power stations, could help to keep national energy bills down, although they are dependent on other energy sources for their power.

Fusion A seemingly excellent energy source. It would produce little radiation and would use up little of the world's precious resources. But... it is proving very difficult to perfect and may not come to our rescue for a very long time yet.

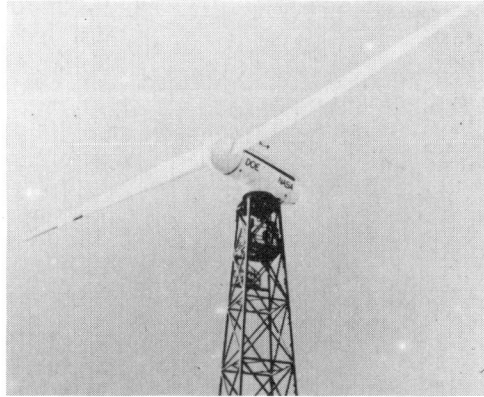

Alternative sources of energy:
Far left Solar panels on a roof in Paris.
Left A wind generator in Clayton, New Mexico.

Far left A geothermal geyser in Iceland.
Left Experimental rafts designed to tap the power of the waves.

Reference

Booklist

Nuclear energy – general There are no dispassionate books about nuclear power. The best that can be offered are the most reasonable, and best informed, texts put forward by the opposing camps. These include:

Nuclear Power by Walter Patterson (Penguin). Covers all the important issues with readable clarity but avoids unnecessary detail and complexity. An adviser to Friends of the Earth, Walter Patterson is totally opposed to nuclear power.

Energy or Extinction, the case for nuclear energy by Fred Hoyle (Heinemann). Vividly written by one of the best science writers around, this book puts forward the cause of nuclear energy with a vigour that at times goes over the top. Sir Fred's contempt for those whose views differ from his own shows through the text.

How Safe is Nuclear Energy? by Sir Alan Cottrell (Heinemann). According to Sir Alan, the answer to the title's question is that it is completely safe. Again this book is clearly argued but without the unnecessary forcefulness that mars Hoyle's book.

Power Corrupts by Hilary Bacon and John Valentine (Pluto Press). The least compromising of all the books mentioned so far. The authors rely mainly on carefully gleaned reports by politicians and scientists to present the most damning arguments they can muster against nuclear power.

Energy – general General books about energy tend to suffer from a common fault – they dwell to a great extent on economics and general complex questions about pricing. Nevertheless, there are some useful texts for those interested in this fascinating subject and its future importance for mankind. These include:

Energy: A Guidebook by Janet Ramage (Oxford Paperbacks). A general guide to the different attributes and disadvantages of each form of energy, presented in detail but without undue complexity. Commended for leaving readers to make up their own minds.

The Energy Question by Gerald Foley (Penguin). A fairly solid, succinct survey of the world's energy resources and their potential for development. Neither optimistic nor pessimistic.

Alternative energy sources Again most books in this category are far from being dispassionate. However, here are some of the better ones:

Renewable Energy: the power to choose by Daniel Deudney and Christopher Flavin (Norton). Described on its back cover as a 'hard-nosed yet hopeful look' at energy alternatives. The two authors, senior researchers at the Worldwatch Institute in Washington, cover all the renewable energy options now open for us to exploit.

Solar Prospects by Michael Flood (Wildwood House). Although principally concerned with solar power, Michael Flood – of Friends of the Earth – in fact considers all renewable options in this illustrated, easily digestible book.

For an opposition view of alternatives, readers need look no further than Fred Hoyle's *Energy or Extinction*.

The international scene
Nuclear Power: the market test by Christopher Flavin (Worldwatch Institute). A fairly dismal vision of nuclear power's current status as a worldwide energy provider.

The Menace of Atomic Energy by Ralph Nader and John Abbotts (Norton). Co-authored by America's leading consumer protection campaigner, the book is a fairly committed denouncement of the nuclear industry in the US.

Additional literature on all these subjects can be obtained by contacting the various pro- and anti-nuclear organizations listed.

Useful addresses

Organizations concerned with nuclear energy fall into several distinct groups.

Most **government and official bodies** can be relied on to be fairly pro-nuclear. They include:

United Kingdom Atomic Energy Authority, 11 Charles II Street, London SW1

United States Nuclear Regulatory Commission, Washington DC 20555, USA

Atomic Energy of Canada Ltd, 275 Slater Street, Ottawa K1A 054, Ontario, Canada

International Atomic Energy Agency, PO Box 100, A-1400 Vienna, Austria

National Radiological Protection Board, Harwell, Didcot, Oxfordshire OX11 0RQ

There are also many **professional and scientific organizations** with a special interest in nuclear energy. Most are ready with information and advice on one or other side of the debate.

American Nuclear Society, 555 North Kensington Avenue, Le Grange, Park, Illinois 60525, USA

British Nuclear Forum, 1 St Albans Street, London SW1Y 4SL

Canadian Nuclear Association, 111 Elizabeth Street, Toronto M5G 1P7, Ontario, Canada

Stockholm International Peace Research Institute, Sveavaegen 166, S-113 46 Stockholm, Sweden

Union of Concerned Scientists, 1384 Massachusetts Avenue, Cambridge, Mass. 02238, USA

Environmental groups are generally hostile to the nuclear industry and support alternative energies. They are usually very willing to help, and many have brochures and information leaflets.

Friends of the Earth (UK), 377 City Road, London EC1V 1NA

Friends of the Earth (US), 1045 Sansome Street, San Francisco, California 94111, USA

Friends of the Earth International, PO Box 7235, S-402 35 Goteborg, Sweden

Greenpeace (London), 36 Graham Street, London N1

Greenpeace (HQ), Damrak 83, 1012 LN Amsterdam, Netherlands

Anti-Nuclear Campaign, PO Box 216, Sheffield S1 1BD

Glossary of nuclear terms

Atom – The smallest unit of a chemical element. An atom – which has a diameter less than one hundred-millionth of an inch – has a central nucleus of protons and neutrons around which orbit swarms of electrons.

China syndrome – The worst conceivable reactor accident in which the core melts completely and burns through its containment vessel, heading down through the ground 'to China'.

Cladding – Containers in which nuclear fuel is placed to hold in its fission by-products.

Containment – The building within which a reactor is built and which holds in any radioactivity that might leak from it.

Coolant – The liquid or gas which is pumped through a reactor's core to remove its heat.

Core – The part of a reactor that contains its fuel and where fission reactions take place.

Emergency core cooling systems – A method for flooding a reactor with coolant (usually water) should its normal coolant supply break down.

Enrichment – The process by which the proportion of uranium 235 in natural uranium is increased above its normal level of 0.7 per cent.

Fast breeder reactor – A reactor in which new fuel can be bred by absorption of fast neutrons.

Fission – The splitting of an atom into fragments, a process that releases energy.

Fuel element – A rod or pin of nuclear fuel (uranium or plutonium) inside its cladding.

Fusion – The uniting – at very high temperatures – of light elements such as hydrogen to form heavier ones, usually helium, a process that releases energy.

Graphite – Crystalline carbon which acts as a moderator to slow down neutrons inside a reactor, making it easier for uranium to absorb them.

Half-life – The amount of time taken for a sample of radioactive material to decay to half its original weight.

Isotopes – Forms of an element that have different numbers of neutrons in their nucleii but the same numbers of protons.

Magnox – The name given to the alloy which was used as fuel cladding on Britain's early nuclear reactors, after which they were named.

Megawatt – One million watts of power, enough to supply 1,000 one-kilowatt domestic fires.

Meltdown – The ultimate effect of a reactor core overheating, causing its cladding and fuel to liquefy.

Neutron – An elementary particle found in an atom's nucleus and which brings about nuclear fission.

Plutonium – An element produced by bombarding uranium 238 with neutrons.

Radioactivity – Changes which occur in atomic nucleii. When this happens nuclear particles and gamma radiation are emitted.

Rem – Basic unit of radiation exposure.

Uranium – The heaviest naturally occurring chemical element. It is the original source of fuel for nuclear reactors.

Index

The numbers in **bold** refer to illustrations and captions

Credits

Atomic Energy Research
   Establishment, Harwell, 28
Martin Bond 34-5, 58 (top left)
BPCC/Aldus Archive 36
Camera Press 6, 40, 59 (top
   right)
Peter Francis/Camera Press 16
Frank Hermann/Camera Press
   37
Ralph Crane/Camera Press 41
Gerard Schachmes/Camera
   Press 42
Don Hagiopan/Camera Press 58
   (top right)
William Macquitty/Camera
   Press 58 (bottom right)
Forestry Commission Photo
   Library, Edinburgh 57
Geographical Visual Aids,
   Ontario 59 (bottom left)
Greenpeace 27 (right)
JET Joint Undertaking 44
Jenny Matthews/Format 54
Bert Miller/Black Star
   NY/Colorific 8
The Photo Source/Keystone
   18-19, 38, 48-9, 58 (bottom
   left), 59 (top left)
Popperfoto 11 (bottom), 13, 15,
   20, 32, 46, 53 (top and
   bottom), 56
Rex Features Ltd 4, 21, 24-5,
   26-7, 31, 39, 50-51
TASS 22
United Kingdom Atomic Energy
   Authority 11 (top), 12, 17, 25
   (top), 47, 59 (bottom right)
ZEFA front cover

Picture research by Suzanne
Williams; design by Paul May.